WHAT
THE
BODY
KNOWS

For Richard Gingrich,
with hope for our journeys.

Jean Janzen
May 2018

THE DREAMSEEKER
POETRY SERIES

Books in the DreamSeeker Poetry Series, intended to make available fine writing by Anabaptist-related poets, are published by Cascadia Publishing House under the DreamSeeker Books imprint and often copublished with Herald Press. Cascadia oversees content of these poetry collections in collaboration with the DreamSeeker Poetry Series Editor Jeff Gundy (Jean Janzen volumes 1-4) as well as in consultation with its Editorial Council and the authors themselves.

1 On the Cross
   By Dallas Wiebe, 2005

2 I Saw God Dancing
   By Cheryl Denise, 2005

3 Evening Chore
   By Shari Wagner, 2005

4 Where We Start
   By Debra Gingerich, 2007

5 The Coat Is Thin, 2008
   By Leonard Neufeldt

6 Miracle Temple, 2009
   By Esther Stenson

7 Storage Issues, 2010
   By Suzanne Miller

8 Face to Face, 2010
   By Julie Cadwallader-Staub

9 What's in the Blood, 2012
   By Cheryl Denise

10 The Apple Speaks, 2012
   By Becca J. R. Lachman

Also worth noting are two poetry collections that would likely have been included in the series had it been in existence then:

DreamSeeker Books also continues to release occasional high-caliber collections of poems outside of the DreamSeeker Poetry Series:

WHAT THE BODY KNOWS

POEMS BY
JEAN JANZEN

DreamSeeker Poetry Series, Volume 12

DreamSeeker Books
TELFORD, PENNSYLVANIA

an imprint of
Cascadia Publishing House LLC

Cascadia Publishing House orders, information, reprint permissions:
contact@CascadiaPublishingHouse.com
1-215-723-9125
126 Klingerman Road, Telford PA 18969
www.CascadiaPublishingHouse.com

The paper used in this publication is recycled and meets the
minimum requirements of American National Standard for Information
Sciences—Permanence of Paper for Printed Library Materials, ANSI Z39.48-1984.1984

Versions of poems in this collection have appeared in various outlets.
For a complete listing, see Acknowledgments section, back of book.

Library of Congress Cataloguing-in-Publication Data
Janzen, Jean.
  [Poems. Selections]
  What the body knows / Jean Janzen.
      pages cm. -- (DreamSeeker poetry series ; volume 12)
  ISBN 978-1-68027-001-3 (softcover : acid-free paper)
  I. Title.
  PS3560.A5364A6 2015
  811'.54--dc23
                                                    2014043472

20 19 18 17 16 15   10 9 8 7 6 5 4 3 2 1

In memory of Louis

"Maybe love for God amounts
to the Beloved returning
the Lover's gaze."
—Li-Young Lee,
"Virtues of the Boring Husband"

TABLE OF CONTENTS

WHAT THE BODY KNOWS

LETTING OUT THE SEAMS

This small study was once my sewing room.
Here I tucked, snipped, and knotted my way

toward perfection with a temperamental
sewing machine and tangled bobbins,

all for the proper fitting. Now
I undo the years with pen and paper.

I pull out threads, darts, and hems,
free the arms for stretching and for

the release of breath stitched tightly
for decades. I expose the belly's curve.

No pins, just words in lines like scissors
allowing the rib cage to expand. Nothing

but a voice in various pitches, trying
words on for fit, even as they

refuse to stay, silk pieces falling,
the whispers of my skin.

I

PSALM 91

Under the attic rafters my sister and I
played house, our dolls naked and stiff
in our arms as we dressed them.

Summer rain drumming overhead,
rumble of thunder. Don't be afraid,
we lisped, and sang into the small

curve of their ears, wrapped the blanket
tighter. Little girls mothering our dolls,
their eyelids closing as we lowered them

into shoe box beds. "He shall give
his angels charge over thee,"
we chanted into the solemn air

of the wartime '40s, "to keep thee
in all thy ways," as somewhere far
away bodies fell under burning planes,

children screamed and stumbled
for cover among the dead, their eyes
wide open under the shadow of the Almighty.

SATURDAY NIGHTS

We piled into the '39 Chevy
and drove to our cousin's farm,
father's sermon notes folded into the Bible
and resting on his desk at home.

We did it for the easy talk,
fragrance of ripening apples, Jake's
laughter and Anna's angel food.
Sometimes a late supper under trees

after the last hay bales were lifted
into the barn, light bulb swinging
from the elm, moths swirling, all
of it floating into Sunday's sermon,

so that the fragrance and wings
sweetened the words of the prophets
the next morning when my father's voice
stretched over us, his broad hands

lifted at last in benediction.
"Bless you and keep you" like a promise,
even for us, the little girls, swinging
our legs impatiently toward afternoon.

WINTER CHILD

In winter Sunday afternoons we lugged
our sleds and toboggans up the hill outside
of town, pushed off on creaking snow,
boots digging in, then the swift descent
with bump and lift. One wild ride after another,
joyful spills among friends and strangers.
A blur now, those afternoons, except for
Mr. Reimer, the mortician, who is flying downhill
in luminous spray with shout and laughter,
arms around his small son. I can see him
climbing back up, panting and unzipping
his jacket between rides as he calls out
to the boy, his voice surging and ebbing.

*

On rare Sundays our neighbor arrived
with horse and covered sled to take us
to church. Plank benches, heavy blankets
over our knees as we lurched and tilted
over drifts. A blind travel—only winter's
half-light through canvas, a small stove
hot with coals, clanking in the motion,
a fire riding with us, and in the horse
as she snorted and plowed.

*

Sometimes when I lie on my back,
arms and legs splayed, I remember falling
backward into snow to make the shape
of an angel, pumping my arms for wings,
my legs for the gown. A kind of ecstasy,
small figure falling again and again
to make a host of angels in my own backyard,
then standing among those glistening wings
before they disappeared into the dark
and the drifting. Now in the night, my body
still, the child looks down at me in the snow
of sleep, the distant sound of rising wind.

GALLOPING

Seven of us under one small roof,
a garden, chickens, and cow—simple
needs in a small town. Yet always, music.
Once a clarinet, the constant piano,
and then a trumpet and voice lessons,
my brother expanding the walls
with his rich baritone until father said,
"No, not inside. Practice in the barn!"
While the cow was being milked,
the "Galloping" song over and over.
This was as close to nobility as we
would come. No hunt or chase of fox,
but the joy of the ride as my handsome
brother leaned into the high notes,
the barn echoing as his lungs expanded,
his throat open and vibrating with song
sounding into the universe, Henry,
at seventeen, carrying us with him.

BULLHEADS IN MINNESOTA

Mother fried them in butter—
bottom feeders that sometimes
tasted like mud—piled the platter
and set it before my father at dinner.

I knew that fish were biblical,
Peter's miraculous catch, and Jesus
on the misty beach frying breakfast,
but these bullheads turned my stomach

and tightened my throat with the threat
of catching a bone, while father lifted
one flaky chunk after another with
his fork, gently removing the delicate

pieces of spine with his fingers,
and laying them around the edge
of his plate, leaving a halo of bones.

CLARINET WITH SMOKE

In our small town, a bandstand in the park
where summer evenings brass and woodwinds played.
A child, I sat on cooling grass, the dark
leaning against the maples, my father near,
our neighbor with his glowing cigarette.
What did I know at eight or ten about
the song of wood, the way an exhalation
bends the breath into keen and call, then floats?
And now at eighty I hear it once again,
mouth on the reed, the hollowed center clear,
yet softened by the cells of wood—glissandi,
fragrance, and harmonies mingling in the trees,
the way my years are now held up in air,
a clarinet holding the highest note somewhere.

REMPEL ELECTRIC

The brand was Hotpoint, rows
of appliances in white silence
as customers were absent,
bound to ripened wheat fields.

Among stoves and washers
I kept the store, still as a cemetery
except the sound of my hand
turning another page

in the Christian romance novel—
man meets woman, plugged in
and ready in July 1951.
No touching, the book said.

Temperature control at harvest-time,
deep-freezers waiting for purchase,
their lids raised above the shining
vault, ready for cuts of prime rib

and breast of chicken. Hopeful
bride-to-be waiting for field
work to end, so that customers
would walk in to examine

the clean, empty refrigerators,
and I could say, "fill," "preserve,"
"defrost," as I stroked the smooth
lines, as I opened the door.

ANDERSON MERCANTILE

Every afternoon the lists of inventory,
the typewriter and I in a cavernous room.
Four hours of bobby pins, pencils,
and band aids. After morning classes—
History of Music and Synopsis
of the Gospels—the keys clattered
lists of trifles. Salesmen clanged
in and out through the doors, weary
of the road, bringing a bit of heaven
to children. A nickel in the pocket
and one could choose between
balloons, a candy bar, or gum drops
falling from the scoop onto the scale.
Trivial and ancient, these contracts
for purchase. This whole world of contracts,
even our chants and prayers. And yet,
at day's end another sunset, pure gift,
as Tony dropped me off at the girls' dorm,
the way he waited and watched until
I unlocked the door and waved goodbye.

ON THE WESTERN PLAIN

And then you came over the endless horizon,
a figure in the distance, stepping over
the sprouting fields and meadows.

You came with the wind, grit of earth
in your hair. You came like rain, shining,
and knocked at my door.

And when I opened it, you entered
carrying the wild
on your shoes and sleeves—

morning glory, beebalm, milkweed,
Queen Anne's lace, snow-on-the-mountain,
prairie violet, shooting star.

NEVER SAY NO

My mother's only marriage advice:
Never say no. Comb your hair,
and wear a clean apron.

Only an apron, he murmured,
leading me to bed. This
after years of say no, say no,

what I repeated to my children,
waiting for the late click of the door,
waiting for the vow.

My mother turns in her bed.
Ninety-five years and she
gazes past me. Yes.

CROSSING OVER

From Chicago to Los Angeles we crossed
two mountain ranges, lightly skidding
against the Rockies in a June snowstorm,
and finally descended over the Sierra

into the City of Angels with her shroud
of smog and two upstairs rooms in a widow's
house. Husband, hospital intern, tends
the dying who call out for their lost cities

while newborns gasp for air. Day after
night after day, I am alone, waiting
for the birth of our child. I sing to her
under the rustle of palm trees and the silence

of the hidden San Gabriel range. Then one morning
they suddenly appear, quite near, shouldering
up above a thousand rows of little houses
and the freeway where my husband enters

the stream toward work. Under their gaze
we are fledglings who have stepped off
the edge, testing the currents, as they hover,
these giants risen from our trembling earth.

WRITING THE FIRE

Child with crayon draws
one line, then another, a curve,
and finally, the circle of O,
a story in alphabet.

Shelter of H for house with smoke
rising. Capital I, the column
on which we teeter, unless
we bend, arms open to the other.

Write it, words that lean
into each other, then pull away
in patterns of flicker and glow
until all is given up to air.

*

I write "Ash Wednesday,"
give title to my body's burning.
Now in this valley's cusp of spring,
first stirrings in the vineyard

where the vintner chose two stems
and tied them to the wire, bound
to drink the roots and dawn, for
the miracle of leaf unfolding,

and for the grape's green kernel.
Write it, that slow swelling toward
ripeness, and the crush, which
we sip and swallow into smoldering.

*

I sleep with Psalms beside my head,
the pages luminous with pain and praise.
My dreams wander in the wilderness
where manna is hidden, and I wake,

starved for the day's gifts:
husband breathing beside me,
my body's power to turn, to stand,
and walk into another morning.

Write it, the hunger and the song—
the bee in patterns of search and honey,
amber and gold now lacing
this shallow river of hours.

SURVIVAL

After Pompeii where the bodies lie
hardened into place, we visit Sorrento

with its cool tiles, curtains drifting.
Evening stroll, and we buy a music box,

Lara's Song, the tune lifting out of
a pair of lovers during war, the little brass

pins pinging in remembrance where
thousands once fell and burned under planes

or volcanoes. Here I suddenly step
back onto the curb as a car roars by.

That driver in the Italian night didn't
see me, the engine moving him into a blur.

Survival, like intervals in a melody.
Empty spaces between pitches riding

on breath or wings, as we walked on,
alive and together.

THE LAST WORD

—*after Frederick Buechner*

And who is this young stripling beside you,
Uncle George bellows from his hospital bed
in Chicago, untamed city of wind and soot.
His white hair in a tousle, he sits up,
surveys us, this man who terrified me
as a child with his fiery preaching.

Young marrieds in the 50s, we stand beside
his rumpled bed above the traffic
on Michigan Avenue, sirens echoing.
In this city my husband is studying
the body's diseases while I read Hamlet
and King Lear, both of us seeking cures.

Lear cries "Howl, howl, howl!"
Surgeon enters with his sharpest scalpel,
pours medicine that kills before it heals.
No rescue without nakedness, Shakespeare writes,
Lear fumbling the button at Cordelia's throat,
all of us leaning into the final word, *mercy.*

φ . . . 36

GESTURES

All my life someone has lifted
his arms and marked the air—preachers,
teachers, politicians, words flying.
Such waving and expounding, so that
sometimes the atmosphere grew heavy,
as though they were constructing
storage space in the sky for truth.

My son-in-law exclaims *"Lascia perdere!"*—
"Let it go, it's impossible!" his hands tossing
certainty into the wind. My mother
repeated in Low German, *"Lote et senne!"*

And yet, music. The beloved conductor
shapes the air. Once in the choir of Brahms'
"Requeim" he implored us to sing
"All flesh is grass," tympani rumbling
into the vast columns around us. I gave
my breath away, gave it away until he
lowered his arms into silence.

TRACING THE HERITAGE

Was it by sea or land?
No one knows how far they came
and went. We squint into the drift
where boats float in the harbor
and a breeze carries salt air,
the scent of a thousand years.

In Haarlingen a small shop bears
my father's name. No information
except the routes within my own body,
that hidden map of turns and twists
given at the summit when ecstasy
spilled into a blind travel, and I
was moored inside my mother.

I trace my name with all its secrets
of ocean and forests, the treacherous
climbs, and wonder at my arrival—
Aunt Margaret walking across a field
of snow carrying a basin and linens.
Blue shadows of late afternoon.
A lamp in the window.

MEETING CATHERINE

Today I met Catherine the Great
on the creek bank where I walk,

a Great Dane who is all
invitation as she presses her nose

into my hand. I greet her
at eye-level, unafraid,

for her master holds the leash.
I tell her that she carries

the name of my heroine, the empress
who opened her grasslands

to my people, saving their lives.
She listens, her sleek body

alert, yet calm, for she knows
the contract: steaks for her hunger

and permission to sprawl over
the entire bed, in exchange

for her regal bearing, her loyalty
to the ones she guards.

TWO FOR WILLIE

1

This one is for Uncle Willie who hid
kopeks in his pocket to buy thin, blue paper
and stamps. And for my father who picked up
the phone in 1956 to tell me his brother was alive.
This one is for the death of Stalin and the slow
thaw, Willie breathing coal dust as he
washed the horses at the mine, murmuring
his secrets and his consolation.
He loved those horses, his sons tell me,
his hands tracing the wounds, the way
he shaped words on paper, ink bleeding.

2

His grave is crammed into the cemetery
by the Orthodox church where today
weeds thrive between broken slabs—
fiddleneck, I think, that yellow curl
opening to breathe, small as Willie's voice
when father died, then mother too, and then
the sun. And still the summer bloom, although
the violin is gone, and still the melody
which someone hummed against his cheek,
an "Alleluia" which the priest now chants
as he swings the censor, spilling its fragrance.

WHAT WE ARE GIVEN

In the photo I am crouched and listening
to three chickens—Rhode Island Reds
explaining the mysteries. They had almost
given up, they say, on anyone listening,

what with the scream of fighter jets
overhead, and the hawks circling.
Here at the western edge of the continent
the ocean's glare reminds us, it's either

fly, swim, or build a mound like
my tribal ancestors. Here, last chance
to learn the secrets of the egg, the hens say:
beauty, fertility, and nourishment,

what we are given to give away.
They cluck and shift their plump
weight from claw to claw until I feed
them, sisters at the edge, softly crowing.

"ARE YOU FLYING TODAY?"

On my answering machine, a hurried message,
"Are you flying today? Let me know."
Young man's voice, maybe a pilot checking
the schedule, wrong number. Or the friend
of a trapeze artist, or an angel watching me
at my empty page, how I laid down my pen
to check the flashing light.

I think I will go with the pilot, the one
who pulls the lever for a smooth ascent
over houses and orchards, then carries me
above the San Gabriel mountains down into
the labyrinths of Los Angeles where
he swings us closer and closer to earth, finds
the open runway, and then touches down.

VULTURE SCULPTURE

He towers over me, standing
on a table beside the sofa
where I read and watch the news.

Bill wide open, his black wings
begin to spread below the naked neck,
ready to float down.

He is starving and I am his hope,
even as my body
still moves and breathes.

Presented as a birthday gift,
he wore a vest and serving towel
over one wing, ready to offer me

my last meal. The book says
that vultures cannot caw,
only hiss or softly groan.

I'll choose the groan, the sound
of ecstasy when our deepest hunger
finds a feast, and we eat.

PLAYING BACH'S THREE-PART INVENTION #9

Bach marks it *getragen*, then *klagend*:
solemn, complaining. Three voices
intertwining in dissonance and harmony.

After fifteen two-part inventions, these
journeys in trio, this one with heavy questions
interrupting the intimacy of two.

Outside the window new leaves play
sun and air like a thousand easy hands.
Buds fatten on iris stems

and finches dip toward the feeder,
then back into the cedar to sing
their long arias. All within the rhythms

of earth and sun, while my fingers
on piano keys walk into the dark,
the third voice, insistent and warning

that love is rooted in risk, our thirst
for the other rising like new grass
easily trampled. Still the wild mustard

opens its soft petals. And listen
to the wind in the cherry tree,
how her fragrant hair loosens.

AFTER HIROSHIGE

Wild the sea, its angry wave
forever caught and frothing.

Wild the cypress clinging
to the rocky cliff.

Wild the sail,
billowed in the blowing.

THREE FOR THE BODY

1

All those sermons about the seductions
of the flesh. Spiritual life, the elders said.
But who could hear it without the intricate

cochlea and hammer, or the wondrous
muscles of lips and face to form the words?
I sat supported by a spine balancing

my head, heart muscle pulsing—home
for the mind, according to the Hebrews,
nest of bowels cradling my emotions.

2

In the Book of Kells the Incarnation
Initial swells with bodies, elaborate
swirls around humans and animals—

cats, rats, moths, and angels sharing
equal space. See the harmony, and how
the borders are pressed by fecundity,

how nothing is fixed, the top curve
of the Initial having burst open, fragrance
of lilies announcing the outpour.

3

Body as temple, the apostle declares.
All around, the courtyards of clamor,
our appetites and aches crowding the doors

while inside, the table shimmers.
I saw it first in my parents' faces
and in the glare of sunlit snow.

Beyond the striving and failures, the quiet
center waiting, curtains parted for entry,
the body's hunger to be known.

TENDING THE OLD TESTAMENT

This summer the old fig tree with dying
limbs still bears plump, seedy figs,
pink and sexual in the heat, the large,
coarse leaves like hands.

And the aging pomegranate unclasps
its deep-orange blossoms into June air,
the tiny green centers swelling
to become leathery pouches of jewels
hanging heavy in October.

David, adulterer and murderer, remains
the beloved king. Solomon's high priest
walks into the Holy of Holies, bells
and pomegranates swinging around
his ankles, while our myrtle trees flower
like Zecharias' angel on a red horse.

I pull weeds, turn the spigot for thirsty
roots, the flow from a deep well where
the water is turning its pages.

WHAT THE BLIND MAN SAW

"I can see people, but they look like trees walking."
—Gospel of Mark

Trees with one leg, walking,
spit of Jesus on his eyes,
arms pointing up to a high dazzle
as all around him a crowd
of sound is becoming visible.

What once was a small rumble
on the tips of his fingers, now
pours into him like a river,
a drenching of light and shadow.

He trembles on this new threshold.
Is he man or tree? And did the Healer
also touch the crown of leaves
which now looks back at him
with a thousand eyes?

WHAT IS ENOUGH?

Summer light lingers in the orange trees,
their glossy leaves etching a coral sky,
a luxurious tapestry over our darkening rooms.
"Save the pennies and buy a farm,"
father repeated as he turned off house lights
in the bare '30s and '40s, his salary
meager, the wheat fields scorching.

*

Berlin, 1948, my sister sits on cargo
flying in with the Airlift. She will distribute
food to survivors living in rubble.
In the Christmas dark she offers fruit
and chocolate, and one small boy returns,
tearfully holds out his pack. "*Zu viel,*"
he says. Too much.

*

What is enough? In his later years
father freely handed out dollar bills,
even to the youngest grandchild,
our four-year-old spending it immediately
on candy. This was July in Canada
where, even if the light is long,
it does not last forever.

NO PEOPLE

*"After awhile I did begin to wonder if
I liked the church better with no
people in it."*
—Gilead, *Marilynne Robinson*

The ones who quarrel,
who drone their complaints,
who feed on old angers.
The ones who worship success.
The ones who argue the fine points of doctrine,
who build fences around tradition,
withhold the bread and wine.

The whole blessed empty space,
pews removed, so that the rental truck
can back up to the entry and begin
to unload the tables and chairs,
white table cloths, cases of wine,
bouquets, and fragrant, steaming trays,
while the van drivers are collecting
the wounded, the homeless, the sick,
even criminals. All of us unworthy,
all of us hungry.

THE BACKDOOR BAR

For my seventieth birthday my daughter
transforms our living room into a bar—
black sheets over windows, candles on
small tables. The family gathers.
She has provided a karaoke player
to fulfill my old dream to sing love songs
into a microphone. I've entered through
the back to croon "Smoke Gets in Your Eyes"
while my young grandson works the fog
machine, the pianist shifts foundations
with jazzy chords, and the bass player
hugs the deep hollow as he bends and plucks,
a dialogue between voice and instruments
about a "lovely flame dying" as I enter
my eighth decade in a sleek black dress
and a tune, another cry for embrace.

RENEE FLEMING IN MY KITCHEN

In the airport I see her waiting
for her flight, and greet her to thank her,
Renee, who has been singing to me

for years, her radiant tones filling the kitchen
as I chop onions and pour the oil,
join her in "Un bel di vedremo"

while I whip the cream, the room vibrating
with fragrance and melody in an alchemy
of rise and fall, fire and ice.

How do I tell her that her long, opening
"ah" of "Dank Sei Dir, Herr" becomes
an embrace of all that we are given,

how Butterfly's "Farewell" becomes
all that we lose? She smiles and speaks
with lilting voice, this small woman

who holds our cries and moans within her,
as she turns now to board the plane,
and waves goodbye.

IN DROUGHT

"And now in age I bud again.
After so many deaths, I live and write."
—George Herbert

Jays squabble among dusty leaves,
the creek is low.
Our well pumps silt.

Roots deepen in the dark,
search the heard clay,
a crack for entry.

I remember the winds
of western Kansas, wide fields
of winter wheat smothered in dust,

how I scanned the horizon
for God's wing—embrace
of cloud and kiss of rain.

The source of the word *kiss*
is the Old Frisian *kusse*—
"to press and part the lips of another."

The root of "love"
is the Old English *lief*
from "belief."

The bud is a tongue
that flowers out of the first word,
which is "thirst."

INTERIOR AT NIGHT

—painting by Peter Janzen

Lamplight throws shadows
over two empty chairs, a plant
with broad leaves, and a wall

of books filled with sentences,
lines written in distant rooms
by a figure alone seeking

the next word. Long vowels
of wonder and grief, open cries
interrupted by consonants,

like a lamp and chair, allowing
a place to rest, to breathe,
and give name to the night,

and to this empty space
which I have now entered—
room within a room,

my own wall of voices,
an echo of being found.

POOL

My gift for his fiftieth birthday,
a Japanese maple, buds swollen
and ready to release first leaves.

After planting he digs a small
pool underneath, lines it
with cement edged with rocks.

This mirror, shaped like a uterus,
reflects the tree as it rises,
the soft green lace spreading

its wings. "Womb," we whispered,
little girls in church singing
the word, that secret place which

under the bare branches of December,
holds the sun, moon, and stars.

"TRAVEL LIGHT"

Command or description, I want
to glow as I walk through my day,

as I drift through the halls
of the nursing home where I find you

dozing in your bed. I want you
to see how I'm learning to float,

the air thinning between our kisses.
And yet, the weight—harvest of moon

and fruit heavy with sugar. In August
heat I lift a melon, smell this long

summer pressed against the earth,
what I will carry to you tomorrow.

MARGARET'S ROSE

She painted it large for a queen
bed, her arms moving in arcs,
the outside petals flirting

with the fabric's edge. Arc
over arc, like the world opening
at dawn, shades of pink and yellow

bleeding freely. And in the center
a cluster of stamen dusted with gold.
The quilters arrived with threaded needles.

How to fasten down a full-blown rose?
So she marked a flow of streams
and waves for their stitches,

and at the outside borders, small,
perfect squares to keep the petals
from falling, as night after night I sleep

under it at peace, covered with
the fibers and pigments of the fields,
and the extravagance of another day.

IV

HEAT

Summer fan shivers the rosary
which hangs from the door knob
here where nothing stirs on its own
in midsummer's curl of parched leaf.

"The sun doesn't go down. We do,"
writes Amichai, tilting toward
his own descent. Whir of fan
since childhood, and I want to touch

my toes to cool linoleum, or mud
by the garden pump as I pry
at the locks of baked earth,
seeking the thirsty dark.

One word at a time for the unknowable,
like the beads which I never learned
to touch in prayer, which the air
fingers for me as the sun

does not set, but I do, willing
to receive the grace of moonlight
in my slow slide toward
whatever stirs for transcription.

*

Chirp of crickets, silent float
of the owl. Daytime glare
dissipates now into shadow,
allowing sight, my small study

releasing me into night.
The grass breathes and cools,
as I lie down on the soft blades,
face-up, as in rehearsal.

What words before my final
silence? What language for
the great arc from my grave
to the rosary of constellations overhead?

Heaven and the highest heaven
cannot contain thee,
how much less our earth
in its burning and greening,
and this house, my body,
which you have made.

SEPTEMBER AT THREE RIVERS RETREAT

The hills parched and silent after this valley's
slam of heat, river beds dry, a small rustle of leaves.

Even then, native oaks spread limbs of glossy
green and drop acorns, their roots drinking

from a secret place. Silence in the chapel
where I sit, hands open, listening.

No sound except a brief scuffle of birds,
and then something small falling between the walls.

A rattling of one and then another and another,
the blue jays storing acorns for the winter.

They have found an opening in the tower,
thirty feet above the foundation, a feast

for another generation, only to be found after
the walls come down. One flutter of wings

after another, one acorn at a time, given away.

SLEEPING IN A LIGHTHOUSE

Growing old is like sleeping
in a lighthouse. We fall into
a calm, deep breathing until
the foghorn blasts overhead

on this rocky island where
the host serves dinner with wine,
and smooth sheets for the night.
Every six minutes the horn,

yet we float in dream,
the great blaring not for us,
after all, but for the young
who dare to leave the harbor

and steer their boats into
fateful currents. As though
we are the threat while
we doze in our losses,

huddled under the sweeping
beacon and its repeated declaration,
like a promise: *You are resting*
on danger, and you are safe.

WHAT TO TAKE

Travel bag is unzipped, lid up.
What to take for the final journey?

*

The giant oak by the creek tells me
she is not going anywhere.

*

Creek water climbs into mistletoe,
something for last kisses.

*

Trip, as in fall? My mother
calls out from a far place.

*

Doctor listens to my artery,
orders an ultrasound.

*

Will my clothes by shredded
or hang from the shoulders of strangers?

*

At the airport my bag slides
through security, light as air.

HIVE

Honeybees hum in the chimney
as they work, nothing deterring
them from their devotion to our home,
not smoke, chemicals, or beekeepers.

Forty years of honey stored
inside the brick flue for generations
unknown, all of it perfectly
packed into tiny compartments,

much like our own gathering
and storing, what we guard like
worker bees fanning the queen.
In a dream the chimney overflows

in summer heat, honey streaming
over the roof. Time to sort, to give
and throw away, I say, tossing
books, clothes, even money.

And still I awaken into disbelief—
my unimaginable abandonment.
O sweet world, your mornings of lips
and birdsong. The deep sleep of winter.

"JESU, PRICELESS TREASURE" IN TANGO

—after Richard Stoltzman and Jeremy Wall

Seventy years I have known this chorale,
the rich four-part harmony like a ship

plowing, full-throttle through heavy swell
as the melody's intervals lift and dip,

opening a chasm of longing. The poem seeks
to fill the space—"source of purest pleasure"—

now to the rhythm of tango: cheek against cheek,
we lean into the beat, clarinet wailing the vow

over piano and guitar, hands clasped,
arms extended, our feet in tandem.

The ship strives toward a far land I've never
seen, Bach and I, in sweet rehearsal

on the deck of the universe, for the time we arrive,
breathless, at the double-bar.

ANNE RISING

The air so thin around
her bony shoulders, you think
how easily she might enter it,

but see how deliberately
she moves—the small slide
forward in the chair

before she places her hands
on its arms. Slowly
she rises, her white hair first,

like a crown. She stands
before you now, her warm
gaze opening the space.

Walk with me, she says,
through the air, to the light.

THE DIG AT MAGDALA

They tap and scrape in silence
here in the village of Magdala—
another wall of stones, a floor
lie open to the morning sun.

Here in the village of Magdala
where all is stripped to stone
and open to the morning sun,
a woman walked away

from all that's stone,
her story now laid bare:
Mary walked away
and followed him,

the story here laid bare—
his wild words, his curing touch,
and how she followed him
with ointment in her hands, her hair,

his words, his touch,
this emptiness an open tomb,
the sun like ointment on our hair,
and on the wall of stones, the floor.

SLEEPING BY THE SEA OF GALILEE

How can I sleep
  unless I fall?

How can I float
  unless I am held?

ST. PETER'S FISH

Waiter lifts the white cloth
and floats it down onto the table.
Stars over us, the lapping of the sea,
the old story of water,
how it rises as mist and falls
on the other side of the world,
then comes back.

Today in a museum we saw
a boat two thousand years old.
A deep dig, and the blackened
ribs now exposed, holding
nothing but air.

Here the platter of fish
is set before us, waiter stepping
out of the steamy kitchen
in this place we had once only
imagined, and now swallow,

so that when I write, my hand
will mark the page with the rhythm
of the sea, our hunger, and the way
he filled our empty glasses,
then disappeared.

WHAT THE BODY KNOWS

Maybe it's the ocean's rhythmic tug
that helps me sleep, my body's own
surge remembering its deepest pulse.

Think of those Celtic monks who
scaled the slippery rocks carrying
vellum and inks while the sea broke

and battered beneath them. High
in a crevice, a hidden stone hut
with cot and candle. The scribe

dips and swirls his quill to preserve
the story—Luke's genealogy,
name after name, letters shaped

like birds in every color, a flight
of messengers released into history.
Each word unfurls the promise,

like Gabriel kneeling. The body
knows that wings, like waves,
can break through walls and enter,

that the secret of the story
is love, that even as we sleep,
its tides carry us in a wild safety.

CREDITS

Grateful acknowledgment is made to the editors of the following publications where these poems first appeared:

Alaska Quarterly Review: "Playing Bach's Three-Part Invention #9"
Center for Mennonite Writing Journal: "Heat"
Christian Century: "What the Blind Man Saw" "Travel Light" "The Last Word" "Three for the Body," "Hive"
Poetry East: "Interior at Night"
Prairie Schooner: "The Backdoor Bar" "Margaret's Rose"
Rhubarb: "What We Are Given" "Rempel Electric" "Never Say No"
Saint Katherine's Review: "Vulture"
Solo Novo: "Meeting Catherine the Great"
The Mennonite: "Saturday Nights"
"Gestures" appeared in *First Light: a Festschrift for Philip Levine's 85th Birthday*
"What is Enough" appeared in an anthology by *Poetry in the Cathedral*

Acknowledgments

"*What We Are Given*" is for Ted and Doris Rempel. "*Anne Rising*" is in memory of my cousin, Anne Friesen. "*Saturday Nights*" is for Dee Smith. "*Margaret's Rose*" is for Margaret Hudson. Special thanks to Peter Everwine and Meredith Kunsa for their help with these poems.

For continued support and encouragement, I thank Jeff Gundy, Julia Spicher Kasdorf, Lynn Baker, Joan Fast, the San Diego poets group, my church community, my family, and Louis.

The Author

Jean Janzen is the author of six previous collections of poetry, a book of essays entitled *Entering the Wild,* and her Menno Simons lectures given at Bethel College, Kansas. Born in Saskatchewan, she was raised in the midwestern United States and now lives in Fresno, California. A graduate of Fresno Pacific University, Janzen

Photo credit: Micha Langer

received her Master of Arts degree at California State University of Fresno. Her poems have appeared in *Poetry, Gettysburg Review, Image, Christian Century, Prairie Schooner,* and numerous anthologies. She has received a National Endowment for the Arts fellowship, and has taught at Fresno Pacific University and Eastern Mennonite University.

CPSIA information can be obtained
at www.ICGtesting.com
Printed in the USA
FFOW03n0723120917
39727FF